To:

From:

Published by Sourcebooks, Inc.
P.O. Box 4410, Naperville, Illinois 60567-4410
(630) 961-3900
Fax: (630) 961-2168
www.sourcebooks.com

Printed and bound in China.
LEO 10 9 8 7 6 5 4 3 2 1

A Bit of Applause for Mrs. Claus

Susie Schick-Pierce, Jeannie Schick-Jacobowitz,
Muffin Drake-Policastro
Illustrated by Wendy Wallin Malinow

This book is dedicated to:

Genevieve Bowman-Schick,
the original inspiration for the book.

Also to Ella, Inga, and Louise,
behind generations of love, art, festivities,
and celebrations both McManigal and Wallin.

And to all the other Mrs. Claus's for the
holiday festivities, traditions, and celebrations
which do not come about by sheer magic.

WE APPLAUD YOU!

Twas the night after Christmas
and time for a pause;
Collapsed in the corner
sat tired Mrs. Claus.

The stockings were crooked,
the house was a mess;
The tree had tipped over–
she couldn't care less!

Her muscles were aching,
her feet were so sore;
This overworked spouse
couldn't take any more!

She'd addressed all the cards
from a mile-long list;
Then received several more
from some friends she had
missed!

With the elves she'd wrapped
presents for many nights through,
With tape on their fingers,
bows, paper, and glue.

When she'd lifted her nose,
turned her head to the side,
She had smelled something burning...
"My cookies!" she'd cried!

She was chubby and plump, quite a jolly ol' soul, From testing each goody and licking the bowl.

At last all was done
by the skin of her teeth,
The mistletoe hung
with the holly and wreath!

Then Santa had cried
as he left on his flight,
"You're the greatest, my dear!
Merry Christmas!
Good night!"

The elves were all sleeping,

each tucked into bed;

But visions and fantasies

danced in her head!

Come next year, no more baking
or trimming the tree;
On the beach with the elves—
that is where she would be!

And then she envisioned
a gorgeous new sable;
With emeralds and rubies
hung down to her navel!

When up on the roof
there arose such a clatter,
It ended her dreaming...
"Now, what is the matter?"

Away to the window
she flew like a flash;
As she tripped on the clutter,
hopped over the trash.

When what to her weary red
eyes did appear,
But the emptied-out sleigh
and eight hungry reindeer!

And the little old driver
so lively and quick,
Was worn out by his travels—
Could this be St. Nick?

"Will you see to the reindeer, my darling?" he said.
Kissed his wife, said "I love you," and took to his bed.

"Now Dasher, now Dancer,

now Prancer and Vixen;

"Come down off my roof,
and be careful—don't fall;
You need some warm food
and fresh hay in your stall!"

"Well done, deer,"
she said fondly,
though standing there freezin.'
Her thoughts then returned
to her efforts this season.

She had toiled all day long
and was covered with soot,
And her clothing was stained
from her head to her foot.

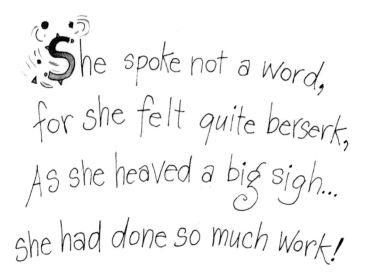

She spoke not a word,
for she felt quite berserk,
As she heaved a big sigh...
she had done so much work!

Then she flopped in a chair
with no breath left to whistle;
A smile on her face
made her finally look blissful!

Mrs. Claus could still smile
as she relived these scenes;
For she knew of her part
in fulfilling our dreams!

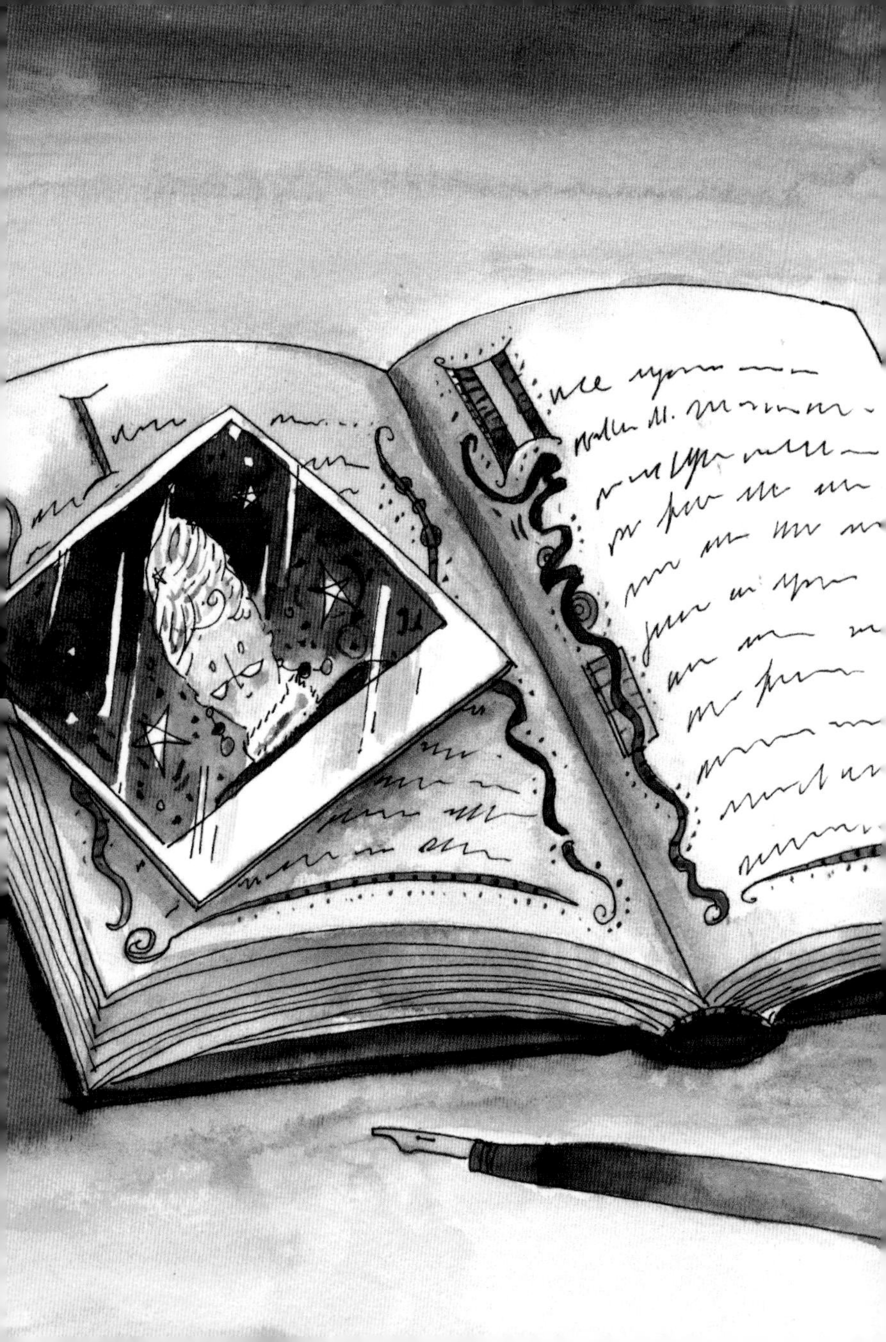

Santa Claus gets the credit
though everyone knows,
Mrs. Claus is the one
who deserves hallowed prose!

So let's give a cheer for our own Mrs. Claus;

Her love and her work rate a special applause!

About the Authors:

Susie Schick-Pierce, Jeannie Schick-Jacobowitz, Muffin Drake-Policastro, and Shannon Drake-Thi are a powerful, collaborative, creative team who have written numerous books selling hundreds of thousands of copies. They wrote and published the following books: *'Twas the Night After Christmas, A Bit of Applause for Mrs. Claus, A Bit of Applause for Santa Claus, You're My Friend BeClaus, You're My Friend BePaws,* and *You're My Friend BeClaws.*

About the Illustrator:

Wendy Wallin Malinow is an award-winning fine artist, jeweler, and illustrator. She has exhibited her work in galleries and museums internationally since 1980 and has illustrated and been featured in numerous published books over the years.